The Cog in the Wheel
Mechanical Philosophy Revisited

3rd Edition

Patrice Leiteritz

This book was originally published in German as
"Das Rad in der Maschine – Handbuch der
mechanischen Philosophie" in 2019 (first edition).

Bibliographic information of the German National Library:
The German National Library lists this publication in the
German National Bibliography; detailed bibliographical data can
be found online at http://dnb.dnb.de

© 2021 Patrice Leiteritz, E-Mail: DRIDM@gmx.de

Manufactured and published by: BoD - Books on Demand,
Norderstedt

ISBN: 978-3-7526-6714-1

Cover design:
idea – Andreas Herold and Patrice Leiteritz
execution – Andreas Herold

I dedicate this book to
my dear wife Christina.

Contents

1 Prologue...9

2 Basic Premises......................................13

    2.1 Materialism......................................14

    2.2 Determinism....................................15

    2.3 The Principle of Causality.................22

3 Conclusions..26

    3.1 Order and Chaos.............................26

    3.2 Coincidence....................................29

    3.3 Probability.......................................32

    3.4 Naturalness and Artificiality..............34

    3.5 Animate and Inanimate Matter..........38

    3.6 The Origin of Life.............................40

    3.7 Evolution...43

    3.8 Man and Animal...............................48

    3.9 Body and Psyche..............................53

    3.10 Free Will...57

    3.11 Reason and Truth...........................67

    3.12 Being and Consciousness...............70

    3.13 The Highest Good...........................75

3.14 The Pleasure Principle....................80

3.15 Good and Evil..................................87

3.16 The Nature of Morality.....................95

3.17 The Fair Society............................100

3.18 Predisposition and Environment....105

3.19 Egoism and Altruism......................108

3.20 Feeling and Thinking....................113

3.21 The Meaning of Life.......................118

3.22 Fate...121

3.23 Religion...124

4 Summary..131

5 Epilogue...141

6 Notes on the 3rd Edition...........................145

1 Prologue

The mechanical philosophy is a world view which is based on the application of mechanical principles to all known processes and events. Matter (resp. energy) is the only substance in the universe and everything in existence originates from this basic material. This also applies to the human consciousness as well as everything mental and emotional. Simultaneously, all forces in the universe interact in a fixed, immutable manner and create an unbroken chain of events. Ultimately, the rules of this interplay are defined by the laws of nature which can be escaped by nothing and no one.

The ideas collected in this book have been expressed by many philosophers around the world. Some of them almost date as far back as the discipline of philosophy itself, others are from contemporary authors. However, because exact quotes and references do not contribute any informative content, they are intentionally avoided. The concepts shown speak for themselves and should be regarded as part of a logically constructed, philosophical system. Therefore, it does not come as a surprise that the individual chapters of the book contain various thematic overlaps. References to other entries which cover related content are indicated by a right arrow ($\rightarrow$). Instead of presenting fundamentally new knowledge, the intention behind this book is to describe the most important information on mechanical philosophy as precise and concise as possible. But its practical application in people's everyday life is not left out, either.

Apart from the intensive examination of the subjects of materialism and determinism and possible conclusions, one of the reasons for writing this book was the current tendency towards esotericism and the hostility towards science in parts of the population. Many people seek refuge in imaginary dream worlds and, in doing so, abandon the most basic concepts of reason and logic. The consequence is a lack of understanding of the own self and one's environment, which, in turn, may lead to confusion and suffering. Instead of distinguishing true from false and gaining real insights, some people blindly believe in the most absurd theories. In some extreme cases, they adjust their entire lives to these concepts.

Certainly, all of this would not be alarming if it only affected the individual person. At worst, however, those beliefs and their negative consequences also affect others, including friends, acquaintances or children. Especially the latter cannot defend themselves against this influence. If applied exclusively, pseudo- and alternative medicine already causes severe damage today, for example by dissuading people from getting vaccinated or by recommending pointless treatments for deadly diseases such as cancer. Homoeopathy, for instance, has developed into a huge business, even without any verifiable impact beyond the placebo effect!

However, the field of medicine is not the only aspect of human life which is negatively affected by superstition. As soon as ideas on morality are based on arbitrarily derived justifications, it is much more likely that they are conflicting with nature. Irresolvable tensions arise between human biology and acquired "virtues" of the individual system of values, whenever such a situation occurs. Without any purpose and without knowing that they do not *need to*, countless people suffer from the contradiction between their natural instincts and an arbitrary conception of →good and evil. Simultaneously, people are prosecuted and punished for basically harmless behaviour in many parts of the world. As opposed to this, a level-headed look on the world in accordance with the natural laws may contribute greatly to a person's happiness and serenity.

The title of this book refers to people, animals and generally every other object as well: Everything is just a tiny cog in the great wheels of the universe.

2 Basic Premises

As indicated in the prologue, the basic premises of this interpretation of mechanical philosophy can be summarised with a few keywords. These are a) the exclusively materialistic composition of the universe (materialism), b) the strictly deterministic behaviour of all its objects (determinism), as well as c) the universal validity of the law of cause and effect (the principle of causality). The philosophy is based on these fundamental principles and all its conclusions are built upon them. Due to their crucial importance, a closer examination of their propositions seems necessary.

2.1 Materialism

Materialism implies that ultimately, all objects and phenomena in the universe can be traced back to different manifestations of matter and their interactions. This includes energy (kinetic, chemical, electrical, etc.) as well, since matter may be converted into energy and vice versa. That means that both are merely two different forms of the same thing. Just like matter, energy can be measured and therefore scientifically assessed. Materialism is the counterpart to idealism which identifies the source of reality in the mind or in ideas.

While materialism considers human consciousness to be a result of a person's material existence, idealism deduces matter from the mind. However, both positions agree in the conviction that either matter or mind is inferior to the other and therefore must have originated from the superior counterpart. This position is described as *monism*. The opposed viewpoint, according to which both phenomena exist on an equal footing, is called *dualism*.

The mechanical philosophy believes that matter (resp. energy) is the source of everything existent, therefore it assumes that materialistic monism is true. The fundamental realisation that hypothetical phenomena which do not possess any scientific background do not exist and cannot exert any influence on humans is very important for this philosophy. This consequentially leads to (an at least agnostic) atheism and a critical attitude towards any insufficiently experienceable phenomena.

2.2 Determinism

Determinism regards all events as inevitable. Everything that happens is unambiguously defined by its initial conditions. That means all events in the universe are like dominoes in a long, widely ramified chain, which keeps on moving without any external interference. Every falling domino knocks down one or more others, just like one event causes the next one. This includes processes not only within the inanimate nature, but also actions of all animals and humans.

One of the most important conclusions of determinism can hence be described as the non-existence of →free will. The distinguishing feature of determinism is the →principle of causality, the correlation of cause and effect, which here serves as the sole explanation of events. Therefore, all events are based on the known and unknown laws of nature and could *theoretically* be traced back to the big bang (and possibly beyond that). However, it is very important to note that neither the actual nor the theoretical predictability of an event is a decisive factor for the question of any event being determined or not. In other words: Events are unambiguously and invariably determined even if they cannot be predicted now or at any time in the future. Human cognitive faculty is limited despite all technical progress, which means that mankind will most likely never be able to predict all events with absolute certainty.

Conversely, a "non-determined" event is difficult to imagine in practice. The reason is not only the fact that we are used to everything happening being caused by certain processes. Instead, there are other arguments against such events as well. "Non-determined" events are occurrences whose procedure is *not* conclusively defined by their initial conditions. According to its definition, a non-determined event cannot have *any* relation to an object or process in the universe before its occurrence. Otherwise, one would have to assume a relationship of dependence which would result in the assumption of an influence by external factors. But then it would be determined again, after all. As a result that means, however, that actual non-determined events would not be bound to time or space. If one assumed the existence of non-determined events to be true, it certainly would not be inconceivable that other events are being influenced by them.

More problems arise from this, however, because this would necessarily constitute an *objectively* chaotic phenomenon. "Objectively chaotic" in this context describes a process, which does in fact—and not only apparently—contradict the universal order (more on this later). If non-determined events exerted influence on other processes, then this would happen completely unpredictably. Nobody could ever predict the occurrence of a non-determined event and the repetition of an experiment, which includes such an event, would be basically impossible. The consequences for every activity demanding a high degree of precision would potentially be catastrophic if non-determined events, which can influence processes in our universe, were common occurrences. For example, if non-determined (and therefore unpredictable) events affected processes in astronautics or the operation of nuclear power plants, even perfect calculations would be useless and could not prevent people from failing.

One important counter-argument, however, regards a much more basic issue: To influence an object in the universe in any way (for example by moving it or warming it up), a certain quantity of energy is always necessary. Consequently, this also applies to non-determined events, as far as the ability to influence objects is attributed to them. If they did not exert any influence, these events would be completely irrelevant, since their occurrence would not have any consequences whatsoever. However, the question arises how an event, which comes literally out of nowhere and occurs independently from time and space, could possess the necessary energy to influence an object in the universe in any way imaginable.

This would only be conceivable if the event was equipped with energy, which must have been created simultaneously with the event itself. If, for instance, a non-determined event caused a window to close, what would be the source of the necessary energy for this movement? If, however, a gust of wind was the cause, the question would answer itself: There was a cause for this gust of wind as well, which equipped it with energy.

As opposed to this, a non-determined event lacks the necessary energy source. Therefore, it would contradict the *law of energy conservation* if non-determined events were able to influence objects. This law states that, even though energy may be converted into different forms, it can never be created or destroyed. Based on these thoughts, it could be concluded that even if the existence of non-determined events cannot be dismissed with certainty, it should also not necessarily be taken into consideration.

Just like materialism, determinism functions without gods, higher powers or other types of supernatural beings which exert any controlling influence. This also distinguishes determinism from apparently similar philosophical positions such as fatalism.

Fatalism also assumes a fixed course of history, but considers fate to be the cause and not the laws of nature. The fate of everything, no matter if it is a living being or an inanimate object, is decided by an universal entity which assumes the role of the central cause for all events. The existence of this entity (in the form of a god or impersonal power) may let the belief in a →meaning of life or in a greater significance of events appear more logical than a value-neutral, deterministic (and therefore "automatic") course of events. The position opposed to determinism is called *indeterminism* and assumes both non-determined events and →coincidences to be true.

From a deterministic perspective, human life resembles a finished movie. The end and the entire sequence of events are already decided even before the first five minutes elapsed. The suspense is created solely by the people's lack of knowledge regarding the events to come. Whether in film or in life: People merely play the roles which life or respectively nature has given to them.

2.3 The Principle of Causality

The law of causality states that every event (i.e. every effect) must have a cause. Nothing can happen without first being caused by an event. However, it is possible for an effect to be induced by different causes.

For example, a tree may be felled by a lightning strike or by a saw. The nature of the cause is irrelevant to the simplified effect (the fall of the tree), because it takes place either way. Furthermore, a certain cause may not only result in one, but several effects at a time. To continue with the example mentioned above, a lightning bolt may also cause a fire besides bringing down the tree. Effects proceed to become new causes and therefore trigger new events as well. This is called a causal chain. The lightning bolt, which was caused by the electrostatic charge in the clouds, hits a tree, which in turn falls and damages a house.

It's important to keep in mind, however, that *one and the same* cause can *never* trigger a different effect than it does. Its effect is predetermined by the laws of nature and unambiguously defined. If this does seem to happen, both causes only appear to be identical on the surface. Lightning brings down a tree once and at a different time, it remains unharmed. Does this observation refute the law of causality? No, because we are dealing with two different situations and with different initial conditions. The strength of the lightning as well as the size and age of the tree in combination with many more factors play a role and influence the result of this process. The results are different, because they are based on completely different starting conditions.

Simultaneously, there is an absolute necessity to all causal relations, which means that a certain cause *must* always trigger the corresponding effect. There is no leeway for any variation. However, it is certainly possible that other causes which additionally influence the process in question may alter its result. The mechanical philosophy assumes that all events in the universe are elements of causal chains. This connection, however, can only be attributed to the natural laws.

In practice, the consideration of causes and effects is very susceptible to errors of judgement. If certain events typically take place one after the other (or together) in a statistically significant way, this relation —which is also called correlation—does not necessarily point towards a causal relationship between the events as well. Perhaps someone goes to church regularly to pray for the recovery of a relative from a severe illness. When the sick person eventually does recover from the disease, one could assume a causal relationship based on how these two processes took place: A person has been cured because someone else asked god to help them. Obviously, not the prayers but the actual treatments were the real cause for the observed effect. In this example, a factual connection between two processes, which did not actually exist, is erroneously assumed.

In addition to this, the cause of an event may easily be confused with its effect, if they do in fact (or just apparently) take place simultaneously. Maybe it is not the excessive consumption of alcohol that causes people to be depressed, but precisely the depressed people who tend to consume large amounts of alcohol and eventually, turn into alcoholics. These are simplified examples which are merely intended to show the structure of these problems. Reality is always much more complex than these kind of abstractions. Basically, however, there is a high risk of falling victim to a fallacy if assumed causal relations are not sufficiently questioned. Therefore, the guideline that a correlation between certain events should never be equated with a causal relation should always be kept in mind.

3 Conclusions

Based on these premises and their propositions, a network of interconnected conclusions can be deduced. Amongst other things, these conclusions concern the view on humans and their origin, life itself, the definition of morality as well as the mechanism of mental processes.

3.1 Order and Chaos

The concept of *chaos* pertains to both static conditions and dynamic processes. This perception occurs whenever a situation differs from a certain ideal (static) or when the actual interaction between objects does not match the expectations gained through experience (dynamic). In the latter sense, chaos merely describes the *impression* of a non-determined course of events, but not the actual absence of causes. Therefore, it can be described as an experience which depends on a person's individual perception, just as in the case of →coincidences, for example. The reason is the lack of cognitive faculty of human beings on one hand and the fact that even the tiniest variation of a process' parameters may alter its result significantly on the other.

If a person believes that all factors of a certain process were considered, a result which does not match the experience will always appear to be chaotic and indeterminable. However, even these processes are strictly determined and leave no room for variation. Therefore, chaos in the static sense is based only on the personal definition of the observer. It is a purely subject-related judgement. In the objective sense, neither chaos nor disorder can exist, because this would result in a violation of the laws of nature. Thus, without exception, *every* process is an expression of the natural order. Whether the respective event also corresponds to people's personal ideas is a completely different question.

A bird sitting on a branch while observing a cross-roads is unlikely to be aware that the inexplicable movements of vehicles follow a clearly defined order. Because it is not capable of grasping the order, the bird only recognises its *product*, i.e. the smoothly passing vehicles, but not the order itself, its origin or its function. A human, on the other hand, is able to understand the course of these events and trace them back to their cause. They understand the message of the traffic signs and know how they influence the behaviour of the drivers. Thus, it is even possible to anticipate the expected events and predict them accordingly. Of course, there is a multitude of processes that people do not understand sufficiently and for which they cannot find an explanation. Even if it cannot (yet) be proven, in this case a hidden mechanism can be assumed.

3.2 Coincidence

People tend to speak of coincidence when no causal connection can be established between the events. This concept is not compatible with the principle of determinism, according to which the universe resembles a perfect machine that works ceaselessly according to rigid laws and produces results without alternative. These, in turn, form the basis and causes for subsequent events. This can be equated with an inevitable order which is exclusively dominated by the causal principle and the laws of nature. People, however, would not have created the term coincidence if it did not describe known and frequently occurring situations.

The *impression* of a coincidence refers exclusively to the human perception. Other than that, this concept is meaningless, since no objective coincidences can exist. A situation in which chance can be observed amounts to a state of incomplete knowledge, because determinism does not allow for arbitrariness. Just because the causes of a single event cannot be identified, it does not mean that the relation objectively does not exist. At the same time, a (possibly divine) providence behind the events should also not be suspected. For this, see also the section on →fate.

Dice are used in many games as simple random number generators. On closer inspection, however, its deterministic nature reveals itself. If one compares a simple game of dice with a game of darts, the result of the latter depends on skill, while that of the former seems to depend on the luck of the player. Why?

The darts player can achieve a measurable improvement of their accuracy through training and is able to play better on average than others. The dart can be directed to specific areas of the dartboard. A dice player, on the other hand, cannot train. The result of the throw is supposedly not dependent on the technique. However, this assumption is not correct. In fact, the two games do not differ in this respect. The person throwing the dice is just not able to influence the dice due to physical limitations. Although the result of the throw can only be determined by the player, there is no possibility to manipulate it in their favour. Thus, throwing dice is not dependent on luck or chance (both terms only describe perception), but—like darts—on the influence of the player.

As said, the perceived randomness is merely an illusion resulting from the inability to influence the event. This is the case with all other events which cannot be exactly understood by humans. The occurrence of an event is always justified by claiming coincidence, although the true cause is the omnipresent causal chain, whose connections, however, cannot be recognised due to their complexity.

3.3 Probability

Probability is also a concept that describes a subjective perception. Taking determinism into account, there are only two possible states for a particular event: Either it occurs or it does not. Which of the two alternatives corresponds to the truth is determined with absolute certainty at all times, due to the immutable course of events, and is not conclusively defined only after the event has occurred. The probabilities mentioned are impressions equal to coincidences, which originate from people's imperfect knowledge. If only probabilities can be given for the occurrence of certain events, these phenomena may also be processes with underlying structures that have not (yet) been recognised. Hence, they are perceived as random by the individual.

Based on available data, the weather can be predicted with a reasonable degree of certainty. The quality of the forecast is directly related to the quality and quantity of the available data. In practice, however, such a prediction does not allow absolute statements to be made. Under certain conditions, for example, the chance of precipitation is given with 65 %, although the occurrence of the event *objectively* allows only the two options 100 % or 0 %.

If meteorologists were omniscient, meteorological events could be predicted with absolute certainty. Absolute *ignorance*, on the other hand, always results in a probability of 50 %, and not only when it comes to weather forecasts. If you do not even include a person's most basic knowledge, you must assume, for example, that there is a 50 % chance that the earth will explode spontaneously tomorrow. Since we know, however, that the cause of this event is non-existent, we consider the probability of its occurrence to be negligibly low and are therefore right. Conversely, nobody would be surprised if the sun rises tomorrow or if an apple falls to the ground.

Both situations are easily understood and their occurrence is certain. That is why we are not talking about probabilities here. But the more difficult it is for humans to comprehend the causal chain behind an event, the more unreliable the prediction of that event will be. From a practical point of view, without absolute certainty only the indication of a probability of occurrence is possible.

3.4 Naturalness and Artificiality

Nature is often interpreted as a kind of consciously acting being and sometimes even as a substitute for a personified god. This also becomes clear in the way some people talk about nature. Statements such as "nature has given the creature X precisely these physical qualities in order to adapt it ideally to its environment" and "nature regulates the population of creature Y by means of its predators" indicate that evolution (as a tool of nature) acts purposefully and has its own "will." This is illogical, however, since this seemingly intelligent approach is merely the result of the laws of nature.

A living being is not well adapted to its environment because it was actively created by a higher intelligence (or "nature"), but because it survives in comparison to other organisms because of its advantageous characteristics which it can pass on to its offspring. Mutations and other deviations from the norm regarding appearance, psyche and physical abilities are numerous and can have a positive, negative or neutral effect on the survivability and fertility of living beings. These variations may even (as in the case of people with blue eyes) become a common feature.

Likewise, life is on earth not because the planet with all its characteristics was created especially for this purpose, but precisely because all those prerequisites appeared on earth which made the formation of all known life the inevitable consequence. This distinction is important in order not to confuse the cause with the effect.

The distinction between natural and artificial things is based on arbitrary criteria. Man has never left the realm of nature and thus cannot create anything that cannot be defined as natural. If one is to distinguish between the categories "natural" and "unnatural" (or even "counter-natural"), one is confronted with a problem of demarcation. If a man-made dam built of steel and concrete does not have its origin in nature, does this also apply to a beaver dam? If a fishing rod is an artificial object, does a monkey act unnaturally by pulling ants out of an anthill with a twig? When a new variety of tomato is created with the tool of genetic manipulation, most people would speak of an unnatural process. But what is it when a mutation causes an animal to suddenly have a snow-white coat instead of a brown one?

These questions illustrate the fact that everything that exists is part of the natural world. If the separation is to be maintained, it is a superficial and insubstantial difference. The illusory argument of the "unnaturalness" of a certain action or thing, however, is often used to justify one's own ideals or moral ideas. This "appeal to nature" suggests, on the one hand, that the supposed closeness to nature of a certain thing is a positive characteristic *in itself* and, on the other hand, that one could separate the natural from the unnatural.

As already mentioned, these are assumptions that depend solely on the perception of the individual human being. They have no universal validity and are instead mere evaluations that are misused to create prejudices.

3.5 Animate and Inanimate Matter

Living beings and inanimate objects are typically perceived as opposites. In fact, however, the sum of the properties we define as life is merely a function of matter. As formulated in the entry on →man and animal, the conclusion drawn, i.e. the equation of man and animal, can also be extended upon. Man is like a plant that germinates, grows, blossoms, bears fruit and dies according to a given pattern. But humans differ too much from each other and the processes are too complex for us to recognise the underlying laws.

Living beings in general are less to be regarded as autonomous entities moving self-determined through the world, but rather as accumulations of matter subject to the laws of nature in the same way as any rock in space. Strictly speaking—and from a deterministic perspective—the difference between animate and inanimate matter is not nearly as great as commonly assumed. Humans only incorporate much more complex mechanisms than plants. And plants, in turn, have a more differentiated organisation than stones.

But no matter if human, plant or stone: Everything is subject to an unchangeable process consisting of cause and effect from which nothing can escape. Of course, it must be recognised that animals and humans (as part of their "additional functions") have the capacity to sense pleasure and pain. In a philosophical sense, the term "pleasure" generally describes the state of positive sensation. Different animals—including humans—are differently susceptible for positive and negative sensations. Most insects feel no pain, whereas more complex animals are capable of very differentiated impressions. Humans have a very broad emotional dimension of perception.

This characteristic allows for a wide range of positive and negative sensations, especially those resulting from social behaviour. Thus, although human existence can be reduced to natural laws and matter (without a supernatural component), nature itself is the foundation for moral behaviour. However, this morality has an evolutionary background and does not have any validity beyond the subjective perception of humans (see also →The Nature of Morality).

3.6 The Origin of Life

Chemical evolution is a hypothesis about the origin of life, according to which the first living beings formed on the basis of organic molecules, which in turn developed from inorganic molecules. All other living beings emerged and developed from already existing life. This would fit the deterministic-materialistic view.

All complex properties that we associate with living beings would thus be merely side effects of the chemical, biological and physical processes that create and control all life. In addition to this, the feelings we feel are triggered by chemicals in our bodies; the personality of humans can be changed by operations, diseases or medication. Nevertheless, it is not surprising that humans have been perceived as beings (partially) separated from nature. After all, in the eyes of many people, humans are governed only to a small extent by remaining animal instincts and are capable of making their own complex decisions. However, it is very difficult to draw a sharp line between humans, animals, plants and even inanimate matter (as described).

All the qualities that define humans can be explained using the principles of determinism and materialism. Rejecting these core elements, however, would cause the common concept of "man" to dissolve and to lose its meaning. The result would be regarding humans not as a singular being, but as one of many manifestations of the universal order, so to speak as a biological machine or natural law made into flesh.

Apart from that, as already mentioned, the term "living being" is ultimately only a term defined by the existence of certain characteristics. Viruses and bacteria often occur as pathogens, even if there are variants of both groups that benefit humans. However, it is interesting to note that bacteria are classified as living beings, but viruses are not. Although an autonomous spreading can be observed in both cases, a virus does not have an independent reproductive mechanism or metabolism and is dependent on the host in either respect. However, both abilities are necessary prerequisites for the classification as living being. Nevertheless, viruses can multiply with the help of a host organism and are therefore also subject to evolution. This example illustrates how easy it is to blur the boundaries between animate and inanimate phenomena.

3.7 Evolution

Plants are living beings, but (as far as known) have no consciousness. But even if, for example, deliberate decisions are impossible for plants, their existence and evolution are subject to the same mechanisms as for humans. If we consider an apple tree, the properties of its components have a direct influence on the distribution and thus the survival of its species. Tasty fruit is more frequently eaten by animals and distributed over greater distances through their excrements. In addition to the distribution of apple seeds by fallen fruit in the immediate vicinity, this allows a considerably greater dispersion. If animals ignore the fruit, the trees will automatically spread to a lesser extent.

However, the plants themselves are not actively involved in this development, as they are not able to do so. The reasons for the taste and colour of the fruit which attract the attention of animals in each case are not a "strategy" in the sense of rational consideration; the tree does not have the desire to spread its species and sweetens its fruits for this purpose. The mere fact that one of the trees has produced sweeter fruits than others due to natural variation and mutation has led to its mass distribution. The evolutionary success of a plant is thus solely the product of external factors and, consequently, of the laws of nature. The situation is similar for humans and animals. In fact, consciousness and will are merely the product of the evolutionary process.

In the development and dissemination of character traits, heredity (as in the case of a person's inherited appearance), must also be considered. If humans reproduce conventionally (and not through cloning or genetic manipulation), procreation and the rearing of children will always have a significant emotional value for many people.

The reason is obvious: People for whom reproduction is particularly important are statistically more likely to have offspring. Thus, the majority of all children also has a greater chance of inheriting this character trait from their parents and is also more likely to be interested in reproduction. On the other hand, the aversion to reproduction tends to die out with its bearers. Of course, this will never happen completely, as there will always be a natural dispersion and variation of personal traits.

Nevertheless, the observation remains that human characteristics are ultimately shaped by the laws of nature alone. In this way, certain patterns of personal traits are automatically constructed over thousands of generations (in the course of time, through the relationship between cause and effect) and ultimately result in more or less pronounced collective opinions. The view of the majority that killing people is wrong has been deeply rooted in human morality throughout the history of mankind, as it encourages coexistence and peace in society (see →The Nature of Morality).

Evolution still offers an explanatory model for the development of living beings. In addition, the example of mankind also reveals a further development of evolution itself. In the case of the simplest beings (such as bacteria), evolution only shapes the functional components of the body. These were the decisive factors for the selection of the best adapted living beings. Later, the properties of appearance were added, which play an important role especially in reproduction. In the case of more complex animals and humans, the first two levels were important then and are important now as well, but social behaviour and personality traits have been moving more and more to the centre.

These are ultimately dependent on the structure of our physical bodies and, like our external appearance, are inherited and then shaped by external influences. The assumption that evolution no longer has any influence on the human species is therefore illogical. It is still of central importance for the development of mankind, but often takes place in other areas than with other animals. Of course, it is not the social behaviour of the individual human being that is to be considered, but rather the average behaviour of entire societies.

Consciousness is created by the body and only appears through it (see →Body and Psyche). The reason for this development can also be found in evolution. The ability to be aware of oneself in conjunction with highly developed faculties of the brain ultimately lead to considerations regarding one's own existence. However, if a person believes in a meaningful life (according to their own judgement) and in their autonomy, the motivation to survive and to have children increases considerably. One could therefore argue that the (false) conclusion regarding one's own freedom of will was a milestone on man's evolutionary path. At some point, however, the day will come when people will give up faith in free will in favour of the truth. And this will at the same time enable them to rid themselves of many prejudices which currently still affect their life.

3.8 Man and Animal

The question of the extent to which artificial intelligence (AI) can be assumed to be a mere simulation of a consciousness or a "real" consciousness is possibly irrelevant. It is conceivable that there is no real difference between both. An AI merely follows its programming, just as a human being always corresponds to their will. Consciousness, in this case, would not be a static property, but a dynamic phenomenon, which can appear stronger or weaker, depending on the being. If the necessary material (i.e. physical) preconditions for the formation of a consciousness in a being are met, the consciousness automatically emerges from these preconditions.

The strict separation between human and animal consciousness must be questioned, since consciousness itself apparently exists in the form of a spectrum.

Some intelligent animals (e.g. monkeys and certain bird species) are able to recognise themselves in a mirror. A coloured dot is attached to their body in such a way that the animals can only see it in the mirror. As soon as they recognise this dot and want to examine it on their own body or remove it, it becomes clear that they can perceive and recognise themselves. This test shows that besides humans, there are other living beings who are aware of themselves. The fact that magpies, for example, can pass the mirror test while other birds are not capable of doing so is particularly interesting.

Healthy humans are always able to recognise themselves in a mirror, but only starting from the second year of life onwards. At the same time, however, those animals that fail the test (e.g. dogs and cats) also possess numerous other characteristics that suggest a consciousness. These include the ability to experience and express emotions. In contrast, plants are regarded as living beings, but do not have any abilities that are typical for a consciousness. Hence the conclusion can be drawn that self-perception—as a characteristic of consciousness—presupposes a certain level of mental development. Once this stage is reached, however, the ability to perceive oneself automatically occurs as a necessary consequence. This is only a single building block that can supplement the construct of consciousness; how consciousness develops depends on the respective organism and its material characteristics.

People are more intelligent than other animals. This has significant consequences for their emotional range and scope of action. Beyond that, however, hardly any convincing argument can be found for the uniqueness of humans compared to animals. In a deterministic view, it is likely that neither humans nor animals have "souls" as they are commonly defined (i.e. as immaterial, immortal phenomena), since they are not necessary for the "functioning" of living beings. This means that it would be absurd to assume the existence of an immortal soul, as it is not absolutely necessary for the explanation of mankind. There is no evidence to support the existence of such a soul. Humans are creatures with a consciousness. However, this consciousness originates from the body and is consequently receptive to physical influences and changes, as is the case with animals.

Otherwise, the demarcation between "soulless" and "ensouled" beings would be almost impossible, due to the lack of a definition. If, for example, humans, dogs and cats possess souls in our opinion, why not jellyfish, insects or perhaps even plants? From birth, humans receive a number of differently pronounced abilities, interests, inclinations and other character-istics. These can change in the course of life, but this change is also an inevitable process. At no time is it possible to control one's opinion or decision freely. Our subconscious mind dictates the feelings we experience, the values we hold and the choices we make. However, the subconscious is not per-ceived as the origin. Therefore, these determina-tions are interpreted as belonging to our ego. This always leads to problems when we perform actions and develop tendencies that are not accepted by society.

Animals, on the other hand, are not culpable in our eyes because they cannot judge their actions ration-ally and morally. No one would, for example, hold a lion morally responsible for a tourist's death if they entered its habitat and provoked an attack. In prin-ciple, the same applies to human beings, who are generally able to reflect on what they have done.

This topic is explained in more detail in the section on →good and evil.

3.9 Body and Psyche

The impression of an existent soul arises from the characteristics of personality. The more developed a being (human or animal) is, the more differentiated its personality traits can be. This has already been explained in the previous section. Worms or insects, for example, have no personality, because they can only perform a very limited range of actions. A larger variation of behaviour patterns which allows complex social behaviour is impossible. Human beings and some more intelligent animals, on the other hand, have personalities that are ultimately attributable to physical characteristics (e.g. brain structure, hormone balance) or their modifications (e.g. through education and experience). Since variations in personality are possible, they are also exhausted through →evolution.

Evolution itself ultimately derives directly from the laws of nature and is therefore mechanically determined. The consumption of certain psychoactive substances can lead to a drastic but temporary change in the psyche, while the existence and course of severe illnesses—such as dementia or dissociative identity disorders—show how personality can also be permanently destroyed. In this respect, it is no different from physical organs. Although it could be argued that the illness only impairs a person's ability to express themselves and not their personality or soul itself, this is difficult to justify. Even in a healthy state, human behaviour is constantly influenced by modification of the physical condition (e.g. by hormones or drugs), so that hardly any point in time can be defined at which the human personality can exist "in its pure form", i.e. without any influence. Even our current mood or the question if we have recently eaten or not can have a significant influence on our decisions.

The terms psyche, consciousness and personality may be regarded as being closely related. The psyche is the "mental" component of the physical body, which presupposes the body and arises from it. The personality belongs to the person and makes them—like their appearance—an individual. At the same time, all concepts are also *necessary* products of the biological existence of man. Precisely *because* humans have a large and—in relation to other animals—powerful brain, they also have a consciousness and the ability to gain and process knowledge.

The human psyche is a consequence of the interplay of its individual components, which do not, however, have their own psyche. It is therefore an emergent characteristic of the human body. According to the well-known quote "The whole is more than the sum of its parts", a completely new characteristic is created.

A lightbulb can serve as a vivid example of the emergent quality of human consciousness or psyche described above. When considered on their own, the components of a lightbulb do not provide heat or light. Only the construction of the lamp and the supply with electric current result in these new (emergent) properties, which were previously impossible and therefore remained hidden. At the same time, these new properties can also be lost again. A destroyed bulb cannot shine any more than a dead person can speak and think.

With the death of a human, their consciousness ceases to exist. However, the death of a living being can only be regarded as its last transformation. Every human being "dies"—in the figurative sense—innumerable times during the process of their life and arises anew in the same place, but with a different quality. An old man at the age of 90 is a completely different person than he was at the age of

10, both physically and in terms of his personality. With every personal change, an old version "died," so to speak.

Death is merely the end of this constant process of change, and here too the components of the body ultimately take on a new quality. There is no substantial evidence for a component of the human body that survives death. Accordingly, our life is limited to the here and now and any considerations regarding a continued existence in the "afterlife" would be futile.

3.10 Free Will

The mechanical philosophy sees the human as a being who—like everything in the universe—is completely governed by the laws of nature. These laws, however, stand in an irreconcilable conflict with the so-called freedom of will. First, it is important to define freedom of will correctly. According to the general perception of this concept, a person has free will if, in any given situation and on their own accord, this person could have acted differently than they actually did. This formulation meets the core of the problem, which results from the juxtaposition of free will and →the principle of causality and →determinism.

It is not the person who drinks beer tonight and wine tomorrow evening who has free will. These are two different situations with disparate conditions, which can only be considered individually. According to the definition mentioned above, free will could only be demonstrated if a person would act differently than they did in a completely *identical* situation. Unfortunately, this experimental set-up is impossible to implement in practice, since one cannot turn back time.

If, however, one considers the principles of causality set forth previously, the choice of another action is impossible. Certain preconditions have led the person to make the (in their perception undoubtedly free) decision to drink beer. If one assumes that all the causes that were at work at this moment would occur again and that all the objects involved as well as the person themselves have the exact same quality, then the person will again decide in favour of a beer.

This is the *necessary* consequence of all causes which are present in the given situation. The decisions of every human being are determined by their character and previous events. If one assumes that another decision could also be made in any given situation, it would no longer be the same person. The determinism of the universe also includes the unambiguous determination of the human will. A non-determined will, on the other hand, would be a contradiction in terms, since a will always has a certain cause.

This realisation leads to the conclusion that living beings are not the actual originators of their actions. Instead, they resemble machines that process the information they are given and act accordingly. Not only is it impossible to act against one's own will, the thought itself is illogical. Every decision comes from the will which is permanently influenced by a multitude of internal and external factors. From birth onwards, human beings react to these influences and act according to them.

The two terms "freedom" and "will" have nothing to do with each other. There is no doubt that every human being has a will. Yet we are not the creators of our will, but its executors. Before every action, a decision of the will arises which we cannot influence. Our consciousness only assumes in retrospect that we have made the decision ourselves. If one applies this thought to inanimate objects, a stone rolling downhill also has a "will" dictated by the laws of nature. To stop it in its course means to act against this will.

Ultimately, however, this action is not an "interference" with nature or with destiny, for this action, too, was only one of many influencing factors. So were the tree roots that influenced the path of the stone. The question whether something is animate or inanimate has no influence on this principle, because all influences are necessarily determined.

There is therefore no objective freedom, there is only the subjective impression of freedom. Whether the criteria for these are fulfilled or not depends solely on the perception of the individual (see also →Being and Consciousness). Even a prisoner can feel free if their personal definition of freedom does not presuppose that they can leave their cell at will. This thought carries a great potential for humans, namely the realisation that no situation is actually good or bad. Our interpretation alone gives meaning to events, although we can't freely choose it.

Every being at any moment always chooses the action that seems to be the best possible option. This cannot be avoided, because even a completely passive behaviour (i.e. inaction) is a decision. And even if the decision made is already regretted in the next second, for the moment it was the only possible choice. The previous thinking, or a lack thereof, is not a variable, but a given fact. We ourselves are not in the position to determine the beginning and the end of our thinking process, although we are committed to its outcome. If we think back to the past, we are often haunted by memories of bad decisions that will irritate us for years after the event and, in the worst case, for the rest of our lives. It is rather obvious that this behaviour, except for a lasting learning effect at best, gives us nothing but negative feelings.

However, this phenomenon is so typical precisely because we judge our past self under false assumptions. Our mistake is to look back at our decision based on our current knowledge and personality. We accuse ourselves of having made a bad decision at that time because we know better today. Nevertheless, from our point of view back then, the chosen alternative was the best solution. If it had been different, we would have chosen differently. It is not absurd to look at one's own person in the same way as our fellow human beings. In both cases there is no real control over the individual's actions.

If there is no free will, the concept of willpower loses its meaning as well. On closer inspection, the reason for this is clearly recognisable. Difficult decisions, which proverbially put a person's willpower to the test, only seem to be a consciously carried out inner conflict. In such situations, comparably good reasons speak both for and against an action, which is why it cannot be decided quickly without the necessary consideration. Ultimately, however, a person chooses the option from which they expect the best possible compromise between gaining pleasure and avoiding pain. Aspects such as moral rules are of course involved, but only in the two dimensions "pleasure" and "pain" (see also →The Nature of Morality).

A particularly dutiful person does not always fulfil all duties impeccably because they are morally superior to other people, but because it makes them happy and a violation of their duties leads to extremely unpleasant feelings, which they absolutely want to avoid. An unreliable person, on the other hand, feels differently and does not have a comparable sense of duty. This difference alone is the cause of the divergent decisions of both people, without them having any choice.

Even the *theoretical* existence of non-determined events cannot be invoked for the "rescue" of free will. As already described in the chapter on →determinism, a non-determined event (should it exist at all) could never be dependent on a particular object, place or time. If they existed, non-determined events would be most comparable to "noise" that does not follow any order. The occurrence of these events could therefore only be completely chaotic (here: completely *independent* as well as unpredictable). A "creation" of real freedom by non-determined events is therefore inconceivable.

The individual will usually is the result of weighing up conflicting tendencies. The (initially unbridled) desire gives us impulses for action, and conscience as well as rational thinking set limits to these impulses. Here both forces oppose each other and the impression of a conscious choice arises in the course of observing this conflict. The physical characteristics of the human being (such as the organisation of their brain) determine the strength and extent of desire, conscience, and thinking.

Will a person that is attacked on the street and forced to hand over money under threat of violence act according to their own will? At first sight one would deny that, because they are forced by another person and would surely have preferred to keep the money.

On closer inspection, however, it becomes clear that the victim also acted according to their own will. Ultimately, the threat of the robber was only one of many causes that influenced the victim's decision. In this case, different hypothetical results were weighed: The will of the robbed person was modified in a way that they finally handed over the money. This corresponded to their will because they preferred to lose the money over being physically injured. Alternatives for action therefore exist in every situation.

3.11 Reason and Truth

Reason is the essential requirement for the attainment of *universally valid* knowledge. Ultimately, the sum of these insights is what we call *truth*. It must be assumed that there is only one truth. Every statement is either true, false or cannot be evaluated because of its logical contradictions or inadequate definition.

The attainment of truth is itself of central importance in the choice of alternatives for action. Good decisions are based on truth, while bad decisions are usually made precisely because the universal truth is ignored, and the decision is instead based on false conclusions. Of course, no one deliberately makes bad decisions. However, the problem arises from the fact that man is not always able to distinguish true from false. There is often confusion which leads people—often because of emotional reasons—to believe in poorly founded theories. This leads to problems if a person takes an action which does not result in the desired outcome due to erroneous reasoning. Of course, it is clear that no one is immune to misjudgement and that human nature is not designed to draw logical conclusions at all times.

Regarding human perception and the abundance of different opinions, it could quickly be assumed that there is more than one truth. However, this is only apparently the case. Subject-related phenomena can only be defined in conjunction with an observer (see also the section →Being and Consciousness). These statements are naturally relative and cannot be considered and evaluated without the respective observer. Nevertheless, they display an objective validity.

This means that subject-related phenomena in connection with the corresponding subject are also necessary consequences of the determined course of all events. Hence, if a person holds a certain conviction, then this conviction is the only truth that is possible at all from their perspective. At the same time, it is an irrefutable truth that this person comes to that clearly defined conclusion and not to any other. It is therefore a mistake to question the truth's claim to general validity. Instead, one should consider why different people who naturally think and feel differently are seriously expected to come to the same conclusion.

Philosophy must necessarily follow the truth in order to be effective. Otherwise it would not differ in any way from →religion. By observing the relevant laws, it is intended to help people in their permanent quest for →the highest good and support them as much as possible. Philosophy should answer the *great questions of life* as accurately and truthfully as possible, even if there is no perfect certainty. This is the claim that mechanical philosophy tries to fulfil.

3.12 Being and Consciousness

All phenomena can be divided into two groups. The first group contains appearances that can be defined without considering a subject (i.e. a person). At the same time, these phenomena can be scientifically documented, such as the law of gravity.

The second group can only be understood in connection with an interpreter (e.g. a human being). In other words, the phenomena of that group can only exist at all as soon as a human being interprets them according to their inner organisation (i.e. the interaction of their bodily functions). Examples are moral ideals or feelings. These concepts cannot be evaluated scientifically without reference to human beings.

It is important that the second group (i.e. the subject-related phenomena) is *not* an illusion. An illusion exists when a thing is perceived as something it is not. A thirsty person in the desert could recognise an oasis in a mirage and thus be the victim of an illusion. Having arrived at the supposed water-hole, its true form reveals itself. The second group explained above, however, is just as real and objective as the first, because the events assigned to it are exactly what they seem to be from the perspective of the individual. Feelings are perceived differently by each person, but this difference is the result of the different characteristics of their body and inner organisation. For the feeling person, however, those feelings are as objectively valid as the law of gravity.

The phenomena of the second group are therefore defined for the individual, but not until the triggering events have been evaluated. This means, however, that it depends entirely on the individual how certain events are assessed and how they subsequently affect them. Even if—of course here as well—the individual perception cannot be arbitrarily chosen, it can be influenced with arguments.

Outside the subjective point of view, all events are value-neutral: Only the person who feels harmed by an event actually is harmed. Only the person who feels offended by a remark actually is offended. On the other hand, both do no harm to someone who disregards them. The essential conclusion of this realisation is that the negative effect does not unfold through the event itself, but through the observer's perception.

No one benefits from optimism more than people who think optimistically themselves. But do those people not lie to themselves? Would it not be more honest to simply acknowledge negative events as negative? This is not the case, because a change of perspective on an event and the modification of its interpretation has nothing to do with the belief in falsehoods. No event is good or bad in itself. That is why people should—whenever possible—keep the positive aspects of a situation in mind.

Consequently, different people have different per-ceptions of the same events. This is perceived as subjectivity. In reality, however, the judgements and opinions of all people are based on their objectively existing, personal qualities as well as the individual circumstances, which are always attached to them and (for lack of free will) cannot be arbitrarily influ-enced. A person can only reach one conclusion in a specific case. This is therefore to be regarded as the necessary result of their decision-making pro-cess.

As already explained, this also means that the sub-jectivity of human judgement is an objective fact as well. In this way, the meaning of subjectivity changes. This redefinition leads to the conclusion that subjectivity and objectivity cannot form a dicho-tomy. Subjectivity is subordinate to objectivity and it is its product. This means that the objectivity of the universe determines and enables individual sub-jectivity.

The question of the most beautiful colour in the world cannot be answered without the interpretation of a human being. One person prefers red, another blue. From the perspective of a neutral observer it eventually turns out that, as expected, both persons draw different conclusions due to their personal dif-ferences. Their judgements correspond to their nature and are therefore objectively *true*. The error is the generalisation of people, their thinking and their perception despite individual differences. In other words, these sentences are inadequately defined statements. If, however, the sentence were to read "Red is the most beautiful colour *to me*", the statement would be indisputably correct. The gener-alisation, on the other hand, is flawed and can be quickly refuted.

3.13 The Highest Good

For humans and animals alike, the main goal of their lives is always to gain pleasure and to avoid "displeasure", pain or suffering. The term "pleasure" is used here in the philosophical sense and refers not (only) to sexual pleasure, but generally to an intensely perceived, enjoyable state. The reason why there are countless answers to the question of the highest good lies in the different (physical) organisation of people. Pleasure hides itself behind different masks, but always fulfils the same function: It triggers a feeling of well-being in the respective organism.

As it will be explained in a later section, there is no objective definition of →good and evil. These terms are defined differently according to individual perception, and it is also possible for a supposedly evil person to feel happiness. Likewise, people can be both poor and happy. After all, what a person does to feel pleasure is completely insignificant. Only the effect of their actions on their own psyche is important. Each event is individually processed and "translated" into a sum of pleasure or pain (pain is deducted from pleasure) in order to evaluate its significance.

For this reason, pleasure and pain are the only indicators of desirable actions. No other benchmark is available to weigh alternative actions against each other. A closer look reveals that pleasure is not only the highest good, but also the *only one*. Many religions and philosophies reject this assessment and refer to their own moral rules of conduct and virtues. The problem is, however, that all those rules and ideals need interpretation, which means that they must first be recognised as desirable. Of course, it is possible that the observance of moral rules may trigger pleasure, but this must either be taught, or it must correspond to natural, mental attitudes.

A generalisation according to which a certain moral way of life automatically leads to happiness is impossible and cannot be true. Pleasure itself, on the other hand, is the only good that has a positive effect *out of itself*, i.e. without further evaluation. A person who lives a pleasurable life according to their own rules is happy as well. Thus, it is for each individual to find its own definition of a pleasurable life and to live accordingly (with socially necessary compromises if required). All other—supposed— ways to happiness are heavily dependent on external factors.

Today, the pursuit of material wealth alone is sometimes regarded as a superficial goal in life and is therefore perceived negatively, whereas in earlier times a large fortune was very highly respected. As a more positive alternative, for example, personal education, overcoming fears or learning new skills is increasingly considered to be the purpose of life. It is precisely the goal of self-realisation that stands above all individual paths as a comprehensive term.

But through social attention and appreciation of self-realisation, one collective life goal was simply replaced by another. In this case the striving for power, possession and recognition was devalued and replaced by individualism and personal development. However, despite the seemingly nonconformist tendency of this new ideal, social expectations can be clearly identified here as well. Certainly, a hobby adventurer and globetrotter is perceived to have a much greater tendency towards self-realisation than a housewife with three children, although in both cases this may be the very life plan that supports their individual self-realisation the most.

Beyond that, the question arises whether each person already fulfils themselves as much as possible within the scope of their possibilities. In society, self-realisation is often equated with achieving some-thing extraordinary or experiencing something unique. Mediocrity has no place in this concept. To expect an average person to achieve "self-fulfil-ment" through extraordinary actions has nothing to do with self-realisation in the true sense of the word.

However, this social expectation leads to just as much pressure as the striving for wealth before. People who used to be satisfied with their lives now find themselves confronted with others who imple-ment this stereotypical approach of self-realisation in their lifestyles and receive recognition for it. This may cause even those people who have shaped their lives entirely according to their own wishes to suddenly become dissatisfied because it does not correspond to the collective ideal.

Of course, it is pure irony that an ideal that sup-posedly preaches individualism and independence leads to a lifestyle which is as rigid and dogmatic as any other social ideal. This example describes the trap which people who find pleasure in the encouragement and recognition by other people may get caught in. It becomes clear that not just the activity itself leads to pleasure, but also the evaluation of the activity by fellow human beings.

3.14 The Pleasure Principle

As already described in the section on →the highest good, mankind knows only pleasure and pain as a basis for the choice of actions. This is also called "psychological hedonism". However, the way in which a person seeks the one and avoids the other is very rational and follows a partly conscious and partly unconscious calculation. Humans constantly balance between gaining pleasure and avoiding pain and always choose the action they consider as the best compromise between the two motivations.

In a certain situation, a person will gladly renounce something that they normally regard as a great good, if the actions necessary also have consider-able negative consequences at the same time. Ulti-mately, it does not matter whether it is pleasure (or pain) of a physical or mental, short-term or long-term nature. It only depends on how the individual person assesses the intensity of the respective im-pulses. This alone influences the judgement and choice of action.

There are almost infinite methods for gaining pleas-ure and avoiding pain. The reason is the fact that people—according to their inner organisation—fol-low different paths on the way to pleasure. Only based on the expected positive and anticipated neg-ative feelings can a person prefer a certain action over another. Which action this is, depends on the organisation of the person. A sincere person draws satisfaction from honesty, while they suffer when ly-ing to others.

Even if someone claims to have chosen a certain action *for its own sake*, this must always be doubted. An action has no universally defined emotional connotation by itself. Only the individual's evaluation gives it this meaning, and this evaluation then forms the basis for the decision as to whether this person perceives the action as positive or negative. This principle applies to all human actions. An extrovert only feels fully alive in the company of others, while an introvert perceives the same thing as stress.

Of course, there are also people who do not care about the suffering of others or who even enjoy it. This cannot be blamed on them in an objective sense, because they have no choice as to what pleases them and what does not. At the same time, one cannot speak of a moral superiority of people who have inclinations that are generally regarded as positive or virtuous. These values are determined arbitrarily, because what is desirable or what is to be rejected is determined solely by society.

However, the aspect of *sustainability* is particularly important in all considerations concerning the gain of pleasure and the avoidance of pain. Some philosophies of antiquity already regarded pleasure as the highest good and this view was misunderstood both then and now. Critics often regard the encouragement to pursue pleasure as an incitement to selfish indulgence that knows no boundaries. However, this is a completely wrong conclusion which disregards the people's rational consideration.

The attempt to exist in a permanent state of (supposedly) highest pleasure is doomed to fail from the outset, because there are natural limits to the feeling of pleasure which also lead to fatigue. After a person has experienced pleasure, it is only a matter of time before the condition normalises. This happens either suddenly, through a sudden loss, or gradually, as the positive effect subsides over time.

If people drink alcohol in moderation, they can use it as an effective stimulant that makes good food even more pleasant. The false conclusion that an increase in alcohol also necessarily corresponds to an increase in pleasure is relatively obvious, though. However, if put to the test, it quickly becomes clear that the initially positive effect suddenly turns into negative feelings. The method which was able to increase pleasure before may not only lose its effectiveness, but even lead to the opposite result. Knowing the right balance in all things is therefore very important.

Almost permanent pleasure is only possible if people can reduce the conditions for their well-being as much as possible. This does not necessarily mean that they must lead a life under the simplest conditions. On the other hand, it is important not to develop *dependencies* on certain objects, people or situations. It is also helpful to be aware of all the positive influences that surround people daily. As soon as a person takes a certain privilege for granted, this good loses its positive effect on the psyche.

A person who is accustomed to everyday conveniences such as running water and a stable power supply will hardly be happy about that every morning. Nevertheless, a person *should*, for their own sake. Because of the self-evident nature of this luxury, it can no longer create pleasure, but only cause suffering in the event of its loss. Only then does one realise the advantages enjoyed before. This principle can be found in numerous other examples.

Even interpersonal relationships can be taken for granted over time and are then no longer valued. The less things a person defines as necessary requirements for happiness and the more consciously that person perceives all the good things that already surround them, the easier it will be to gain pleasure again and again. That is the key to lasting joy.

The moderate generation of pleasure (e.g. through sufficient, but not excessive time for hobbies) and the avoidance of pain keeps happiness on a stable level. Often, much suffering arises from the (futile) pursuit of a supposedly great good. But it is important to act as far-sighted as possible, to weigh all important factors and to question one's goals regularly.

The gain in momentary pleasure can, under certain circumstances, lead to considerable disadvantages in the long term. Although a spontaneous love affair may be very tempting for some people, the long-term effects can potentially be much more severe than the short-term rush triggered by a fling. If a person lacks foresight, they can easily decide to take action that they will later regret.

3.15 Good and Evil

The argument of the advocates of free will that without free will, no one could be held responsible for their actions and hence the basis of our jurisdiction would be invalidated is only superficially correct. Indeed, one cannot hold people responsible for their actions without believing in free will. The reason is the fact that something like *absolute* responsibility becomes impossible without free will. At the same time, there is a *relative* responsibility which takes the law of causality into account. A person who commits a murder is responsible in the relative sense because this act was an effect of their actions. This is true even if, in the absence of free will, that person was unable not to commit the murder. Similarly, a falling stone is also responsible for the death of a human being, because it hit them (of course without *"wanting"* it).

But even if the person in the first example *wanted* to commit the murder (and this is always the case when it actually happens), this will is a necessary consequence of personal qualities and the accompanying conditions. Since human beings are subject to their own will as well as to the laws of nature, one cannot speak of an absolute responsibility or culpability. The same applies to the contrast between good and evil in the objective sense. If one rejects these two categories from a philosophical perspective (and rightly so), then all moral value systems with an absolute claim to validity lose their basis.

Beyond the subjective perception, all human actions are merely fixed results of the unfolding processes and thus neutral in terms of value. We define our personal actions as the result of our—subjectively— free decision-making process. But how the process that leads to this or that decision works is completely unclear to us. Of course, we can name reasons that led us to make the respective choice. However, this is also a causal process.

The unambiguous determination of human characteristics and actions goes hand in hand with the determination of the reactions of the outside world and
ultimately also with the *change* of human qualities
and traits. Every human being naturally tends towards one direction or the other, but in the end they
take exactly those actions which calm their conscience and at the same time correspond to their
personal ideas of justice. The personal predisposition can be influenced by education, but this education has a different effect on each person. Success
cannot be expected in every case.

Although no one can actively opt for or against being a serial killer, we condemn and punish them for
their actions. This makes sense in the context of our
own perception. Although a person can reflect on
their actions, this only happens within the framework
of their given capabilities. And since they cannot
possibly be held responsible for these shortcomings
(because those cannot be influenced), the situation

is the same. Characteristics such as "guilt" or "inno-cence" thus exist only in the perception of the human being.

On the other hand, the punishment of a criminal can also be classified as a deterministic consequence, since the judging instances also do not have free will. In addition, punishment serves a purpose and can generate *benefits* for society. Even if punishments cannot undo an act and thus do not offer the possibility of reparation, the perpetrator or other people can still be prevented from committing similar acts.

Ultimately, every person weighs all the positive and negative consequences of an action from their point of view and then decides whether or not to take action. Because people are basically able to think about the consequences of their behaviour, a punishment can in fact prevent a certain action. In contrast, it is hopeless to punish a broken car by beating it.

A *stable* society is governed by laws whose origin can be traced back to human reason. This means that its purpose is recognised by most of the population and that this legislation is accepted as sufficiently well-founded. Constructive behaviour should be rewarded, while harmful actions must be punished. In human societies, the punishment of murder is widespread precisely because it is universally understood. Other laws with less obvious justifications are also less consistently observed in practice. Of course, the nature of the punishment is as well a factor influencing compliance with the law.

In principle, however, all laws that punish acts which are harmless to third parties should be re-examined. In such cases, it is reasonable to suspect that it was not the well-being of society as a whole or of individuals in particular that was decisive for their enactment, but a prejudice. Prohibitions and penalties must be proportionate and have practical social benefits. Only in this way can they be legitimate.

However, all of this still has nothing to do with morality in the objective sense. Ultimately, it must be clear that good and evil are always defined by society. The reason is the fact that these terms do not describe objective truths, but subjective judgements. Only society defines virtues and vices and resorts to either traditional customs or systems such as religions or political convictions. A person whose individual values, due to their natural organisation and personality, correspond to the values of their society, has significant advantages. In this case, they will perceive the laws as just and the customs as reasonable. This person can live their life relatively undisturbed, because everything they want to do is allowed and their actions do not have any negative consequences.

However, if a person's values differ too much from the guiding principles of society, they will constantly come into conflict with the law and will not be able to lead a "moral life" (according to the views of society). Even if neither of those two people is responsible for their own situation, both must live with the consequences of the relationship between their views and those of society.

With regard to the relationship of dependence between morals and a society that defines them, almost infinite variations are conceivable. While paedophilia was partly accepted or even advocated in ancient Greece, it is universally abhorred and punished by law in today's Western societies. Similarly, in earlier times there was nothing reprehensible about keeping slaves, whereas this would be unthinkable today. It was not until the last century that the right of women to vote prevailed in Europe, while the abolition of this right would now be completely unacceptable in the majorities' view. These examples clearly show that the question of good and evil or right and wrong does not depend on eternal truths, but on people's opinions that change over time.

An important insight from the above is the fact that personal happiness is in principle attainable for every human being, both "good" and "evil". In order to be happy, it is only necessary to take those actions which provide pleasure and to refrain from those which cause pain. This, however, relates to an inner attitude, which allows a value to be recognised in the events and actions. This attitude could simply be called *optimism*. For people with a serious illness such as depression, this is of course difficult or even impossible.

The above statement, however, should be understood in the way that one does not have to be "virtuous", "good" or "just" in the eyes of others in order to be happy. Ultimately, this is only important if a person considers the conformity of their actions with the ideals of society as a prerequisite for happiness. However, achieving happiness is much more diffi- cult for a person who thinks and acts in conflict with the values of society. This person would first have to advocate their own (socially considered "bad") ac- tions. This would free them of their bad conscience. But even then, their actions would still be punished by society. This too is justified from the perspective of society, since otherwise the prosperity of one would lead to the harm of the other. The "good" per- son suffers in an "evil" society and vice versa. Ulti- mately, however, the definition of what is good and what is evil depends on the view of the majority.

3.16 The Nature of Morality

For thousands of years, countless people have dealt with moral considerations, both theoretically and systematically. *Ethics* even constitutes a philosoph- ical discipline in its own right. Considering the state- ments made so far, we must ask ourselves what is meant by the phenomenon of "morality" from the point of view of mechanical philosophy and what significance it has for human beings.

The origin of moral convictions lies in the permanent social exchange within societies and thus in →evolution. The values and norms that emerged from this exchange are closely linked to the emotions that living beings have developed in the course of evolution. In fact, moral systems can be seen as a further development of emotional impressions. Humans in particular use moral concepts because they have the necessary prerequisites to understand them.

In addition to purely practical, obviously comprehensible reasons, morality is another aspect that humans take into account when evaluating their actions. These are supposedly influences that exist for their own sake. The consideration or non-observance of moral values in the choice of actions is based on a calculation that is just as systematic as the choice of the actual goal of the action. In other words, although a person could, for example, obtain a large amount of money by stealing, they may be discouraged from the act because of moral considerations. Thus, the functioning of morality is seemingly at odds with the concept formulated in the chapter on →the pleasure principle. On closer examination, however, this assessment is not correct, since compliance or non-compliance with moral rules also has an influence on the human psyche. In the above example, the expected pain caused by disregarding the moral rule simply outweighs the expected gain in pleasure from the money in the individual's evaluation. This principle is explained in more detail in the chapter →Egoism and Altruism.

Mechanical philosophy assumes that there are *no* objective moral facts that apply independently of a person's evaluation. Although a person can act morally right or wrong, this assertion is only possible with the inclusion of a certain point of view. This can be the acting person himself, another person or a group. The view of the respective individual or group thus serves as a standard for evaluating different actions. Beyond that, however, there is no objective basis for evaluation. As already explained in the chapter on →good and evil, all moral judgements are created by people and can therefore only be considered in the context of subjective perceptions.

The "common core" of moral systems from different cultures consists of rules that support the coexistence of people in communities, i.e. that help to avoid conflicts and ensure the health and survival of the group. Inbreeding in humans is morally taboo because there is a higher risk that the child conceived in this way will suffer from hereditary diseases. This, in turn, would weaken the community, which is a disadvantage in the competitive struggle for survival. Society's condemnation of inbreeding thus carries an evolutionary advantage that persists and becomes more entrenched because of the mechanisms of heredity. Similarly, cooperative be-haviours are considered "moral" because they also help to ensure the success of the group.

The moral sensations ingrained in the human being alone are the triggers of actions that, *in addition* to the pleasure gain of the individual, also serve the achievement of practical goals of the collective. Without the link to the pleasure sensations of the in-dividual, however, a moral action would be im-possible, since no one would be able to recognise any value in it. People thus act according to moral rules either if they accept the underlying values as correct themselves, or if they—e.g. in a differently thinking mainstream society—merely want to avoid the conflicts that would result from disregarding the rules.

However, this approach shows that morality is just another mechanism of nature. It does not conceal any higher goal than that which the majority of all living beings pursue anyway: To stay alive and pro-create. Due to the circular nature of all biological existence (emergence — reproduction — death), however, these goal are not suitable justifications for a →meaning of life. The justification of all moral rules that are ostensibly based on *objective* facts is questionable from this point of view.

3.17 The Fair Society

The insights of mechanical philosophy not only have significant effects on the life of the individual, but also on the evaluation of society. In addition to the reformation of the judiciary described in a previous chapter, this especially applies to questions of distributive justice. Without free will, differences in people's property can no longer be justified if the goal of a just society is pursued at the same time.

The economic status of a human being depends on numerous factors, all of which are not subject to their will. No one can choose their intelligence or physical capacity at their discretion. Of course, a person can learn or train something new to develop their skills, but even this cannot be deliberately controlled. Both the capacity to learn something at all and the motivation to do it in practice are given by nature. For many people, the course that will determine their future economic status is already set at school.

With luck, a person has the ability and diligence to achieve a good qualification. On this foundation, studies or vocational training may also be successfully completed. Good initial conditions ensure positive results, which in turn create good starting conditions for further, positive developments. In societies as we know them, the principle *"To those who have, more will be given"* often applies. In contrast, a student with poorer performance will have correspondingly lower chances of getting a good job. This principle even applies over generations, as children from socially disadvantaged families have little chance of social advancement, even as adults.

But what must be the consequence of these findings? The complete decoupling of performance and the economic status of the individual would be the most consistent measure to do justice to these circumstances. This corresponds to the utopian ideal *"From each according to his ability, to each according to his needs"*. The mere feasibility of implementing this model in reality is questionable and impossible, at least in this day and age.

Just as a society must punish harmful behaviour in order to discourage similar behaviour, it also needs a certain degree of inequality in order to preserve itself. No human being thinks completely rationally and will accept absolute economic equality while at the same time people have a varying capability and readiness to perform. The self-serving economic activity in today's capitalist systems is (still) the most important psychological motivation for ensuring productivity. So even if one assumes that the conclusions of mechanical philosophy are correct, the laws must be recognised by most people. The latter must be accomplished in order to establish the legitimacy of the state. It is possible that a complete equalisation of human living conditions will never be implemented, because otherwise productivity and acceptance cannot be maintained.

Since the collapse of a state is, from a practical point of view, always to be considered more negative than a certain degree of social inequality, this compromise must be accepted. What is possible, however, is the drastic reduction of social inequality through the regulation of excessive wealth of the richest people while ensuring an adequate, minimum standard of living for all members of society, which at least mitigates the tendency towards increasing economic inequality. Anything else would increase the natural inequality among people, to the detriment of large sections of the population.

The attempt to create an economic balance in society is often rejected by its opponents as a mere ideology and regarded as a danger to human freedom. Meanwhile, however, it is precisely the belief in free will itself that is an ideology leading people to draw false conclusions. Societies that are culturally and politically very libertarian pretend that anyone can become wealthy.

According to this conviction, people only need to have the determination and must be willing to work hard for it. Both would lie in their hands. Theoretically, it is true that *a dishwasher can become a millionaire*, but from a practical point of view only a tiny fraction of the population can succeed. At the same time, however, the myth is upheld and anyone who is not successful is accused of a weak will and a lack of commitment. In the worst case, unsuccessful people adopt these ideas and constantly suffer from feelings of guilt and self-recrimination. However, it is precisely the lower classes that must work hardest for their meagre income.

3.18 Predisposition and Environment

The question is often asked to what extent the actions and personality of a person are influenced by a) their predisposition, i.e. their genetic make-up, and b) their environment, i.e. external factors. Considering determinism, however, this question is largely to be regarded as irrelevant. Both hereditary predispositions and all events that affect people are necessary and immutable elements of a personal biography. Thus, for example, a genetic susceptibility to diabetes is just as characteristic for an individual as an early childhood developmental disorder, which is caused by the negligent behaviour of their parents. There is (as a result) no significant difference between the two influencing factors. The living being as a material entity is inseparably connected with its temporal and spatial context. In other words, no being could exist in the same form in another context. Even identical twins necessarily grow up to be two different people, even if both have the same genetic preconditions and are even born almost simultaneously.

The appearance of a plant is also defined by two sources: Its predisposition (seeds) and external circumstances (location). Depending on sunlight, soil and climate, two specimens of the same plant can have large leaves and short roots (in the valley) and a much smaller growth and much stronger roots (in the mountains). Despite the same predisposition, it is the environment that radically changes the appearance of the flower. At the same time, two plants with different predispositions can thrive or die at the same location. Neither of the two influences is more important than the other.

Every human being goes through their own development, which is itself necessary and without alternative. Disabilities and birth defects are also included in this, since they are natural to the individual person, or they are are inflicted in the course of their life and thus are inevitably connected to them. If one regards every single person as an individual, their characteristics can no longer be judged. Only in comparison with others do these characteristics appear to be flaws or advantages. In reality, however, it is completely impossible that a specific person could exist in any other way (i.e. without disability).

As has already been explained, it is of course possible to influence people through education. Ultimately, however, it is not possible to consciously control how this education—given the abundance of all external influences—will take effect. Thus, a certain method of education can lead to the desired result with one person but can have the opposite effect with another. This is a consequence of the diversity of the human character.

3.19 Egoism and Altruism

Ultimately, all human actions are motivated by egoism. However, this is not a morally reprehensible form of selfishness (which could not be justified anyway, see →Good and Evil), but the natural and inevitable attitude of every biological organism. The mere fact that different actions have varying effects on different people leads to the result that each person strives for their personal happiness in an individual way. However, the basic rule is always the same: Pleasant things are maximised, while unpleasant things are minimised (see →The Pleasure Principle).

Although, for example, supporting other people is considered an altruistic act, it is the effect of the action on the individual that decides whether the action is taken or not. Both the positive feeling of a certain action and the negative feeling of inaction ("bad conscience") could be decisive for the realisation of the action. However, an act perceived as positive by a single person does not necessarily have to be considered "good" by society. The individual attitude towards all conceivable alternatives for action results in our personality.

Consequently, these features defining the individual must also contain *motivation*, which is very often regarded as something that a person can give themselves. In contrast to many human characteristics, whose inability to be influenced seems to be generally accepted, initiative and motivation are perceived as a product of willpower. However, this is unjustified, because a person cannot motivate themselves volitionally to do something. Instead, they have no part in determining which actions provide positive feelings and which do not.

Therefore, a person only has a problem with killing another person for their own benefit because the negative effects of murder would be too severe on their own well-being. This includes both internal (feelings of guilt) and external (acts of revenge, punishment) consequences.

Psychopaths do not necessarily inflict suffering on other people because they enjoy it themselves, but because their consciences do not prevent them from doing so and they feel neither compassion nor remorse. In their consideration, the suffering of other people resulting from their own actions does not play any role, since they are not able to adequately assess the negative effect. They suffer from a severe personality disorder, although the transitions between mere personality traits and actual illnesses are fluid. An illness is always spoken of when the condition in question causes suffering, either for the person themselves or for their fellow human beings. In this respect, the definition is again relative.

From an isolated perspective, almost every person will perceive an increase in money as positive and desirable. This changes, however, as soon as the money is tied to conditions and used as a bribe. Particularly honest people are very likely to reject these offers, as the positive increase in money cannot compensate for the negative effects of bribery (especially feelings of guilt). However, corrupt people do not feel remorse in this respect and are therefore much more willing to accept bribes. How a person reacts, however, does not depend on a conscious decision of the will, but on their inner qualities. The result is already determined before the situation even occurs. People are just not aware of this.

Even if a person claims to not just pursue their own desires or to devote their life to a higher cause (for example through public welfare, religious activity or research), this is only partially true. If someone helps another person, then this person will of course really be supported. But besides a practical effect, every action also effects the psyche of the person who performs it. If someone commits themselves to others for the rest of their lives and helps them, it is obvious that this activity has a positive psychological effect. Whether a person enjoys helping others depends on their disposition and education. The satisfaction drawn from the action is crucial to whether it is repeated in the future. Thus, other people are helped, but this circumstance is insignificant for the respective choice of action. Practical help is therefore a mere by-product. The motivation for the action arises from the individual, psychological effect that is triggered by it.

From this perspective, the action itself appears as a mere tool to trigger a positive state of mind and is not an end in itself. At the same time, the (objective) moral neutrality of human action becomes clear as everyone is ultimately pursuing the same goal. A monk who chooses an abstinent and modest life seems to draw more satisfaction from this situation than he expects from an average life with the usual amenities. If this were not the case, he would not have chosen his path. This has nothing to do with willpower, but only with the always individual path to a happy life.

3.20 Feeling and Thinking

Feelings do not exist for their own sake and have no supernatural origin but fulfil a concrete function. The emotional sensitivity of a human being is a complex system received through evolutionary processes. It is based on social interaction in human societies and helps to facilitate cooperation between people and thus ensure their survival. The importance of emotions goes far beyond the mere act of reproduction.

If parents love their children and are interested in their well-being, their chance of survival improves and, accordingly, their prospects of successfully re-producing themselves. At the same time, people with a strong sense of empathy find it easier to deal with their fellow human beings and act diplomatic-ally. The social sphere is an area of human life whose customs, traditions and behaviour are shaped by emotion.

In addition to rational thinking, emotions contribute essential impulses that influence our decisions. Upon closer inspection, it becomes clear that the ra-tionality of the human being ultimately serves only to achieve the goals defined by feelings. Emotions thus give people their will (goal) and through think-ing, the best actions are determined in order to fulfil that will (path). Of course, feelings also play a role in the choice of action, since every action always has an effect. Every single effect may ultimately influence the greater goal, the human's physical and psychological well-being. The positive feeling of pleasure is →the highest good, and, as already explained, the criterion for the evaluation of actions.

The common assumption that feeling and thinking represent comparably strong, but opposite forces within the human assessment process is not confirmed. Thinking is subject to the will, but the will is directed by emotion like a flag by the wind. The basic principle applies, as repeatedly mentioned in this book: "We want what pleases us." People are only happy because they *feel* happy. Similarly, something is only important to a person if it is either directly beneficial to pleasure or a means to an end.

Of course, one's own mood and well-being are not subject to direct human control. Just as a person cannot prevent dying from a serious injury, emotional pain cannot simply be made to disappear. In both cases, the personal will to gain pleasure stands in opposition to the actual sensation. A person cannot change this reality, they can only try to influence it positively. Of course, feeling guilty for one's own bad condition is counterproductive. However, it is possible to alleviate negative feelings in the same way that physical pain can be treated.

A previously mentioned method is benevolent thinking about one's own situation by viewing it from a different perspective and the realistic assessment of the *actual* extent of the negative sensation. This could be summarised as *optimistic thinking*. Of course, this does not imply a prayer-like repetition of "magical" formulas, which are supposed to create the good things in life automatically. The advice for optimistic thinking is based solely on the fact that the psychological effect of an event is never intrinsic to the event itself, but only arises through interpretation in the consciousness of the observer. So, if one is convinced that they *must* feel bad when a certain event occurs, then the expected negative effect will also occur. If a person instead considers the situation neutrally and accepts its effects as given, then this also minimises the negative effects on their own well-being.

To be happy, one does not have to suppress or compulsively control their feelings. The critical questioning of the experienced feelings as well as the analysis of one's own ego already offers an essential help to recognise (negative) patterns and to work on limiting their effects. The prerequisites for one's own satisfaction should always lie in the hands of the individual. This means, for example, that a person's own well-being should not be made dependent on the opinions of other people, which can obviously be influenced less than their own opinion. Apart from that, the "standard therapy" for negative feelings consists of the identification and practice of *pleasurable* actions. These suggestions are not a guarantee for improving well-being, but more than that is generally not necessary for personal happiness. Often the problem is that people tell themselves that they cannot reach it; in many cases, they would only have to stretch out their hand and take it.

3.21 The Meaning of Life

From a factual point of view, a human's purpose in life is merely to satisfy needs that they would not have if they did not exist. The two elementary components of these needs are a) the pursuit of happiness, and b) the avoidance of suffering. These are the standards of →the highest good. The section on →the pleasure principle provides information about the way in which people achieve happiness.

People are not completely rational beings. While they may pursue some of their short-term goals in a very rational manner, their life as a whole does not follow a purposeful strategy for achieving an *objectively* justifiable life goal. Instead of steering their whole life in a certain direction, they focus on parts of it (e.g. family, career, hobby). The reason is simple: There is no objective, primary goal in life.

All imaginable goals are merely options that coexist equally. Only the interpretation of the individual raises one goal above another. For religious people, it is their individual faith that defines their higher goals in life. The same applies, however, to political, moral and other systems that can assume such a function. In any case, people only have one option: they declare an arbitrary, subjective ideal as their personal purpose in life. In contrast to humans, simpler animals have no way of thinking about their whole lives. Short-term goals are therefore sufficient to justify the continuous action of the animal. The "main goal" of life is not questioned and therefore does not have to be defined.

A human has no duty in life to fulfil and no goal to achieve. It can be assumed that death represents an absolute end of existence. This means that upon death, all events and actions in life lose their meaning. No potential goal in life is of objective importance, therefore nothing needs to be achieved, learned or attained. Every human is born and every human dies. At first glance, this assessment can have a disappointing effect, due to the obvious "futility" of life.

From another, optimistic point of view, it opens unlimited possibilities for the individual. Nothing is fixed, everything is allowed. There is no "last judgement." The only responsibility there is must be borne during one's lifetime. Nobody has the monopoly on morally correct actions. There are only worldly authorities who rule over nothing but a microscopic part of material existence. The universe is of unimaginable size and the individual person is completely unimportant and no supernatural burden rests on their shoulders. What could be more liberating?

3.22 Fate

Fate is a term that can easily be misunderstood. In the context of mechanical philosophy, one could speak of fate to describe the necessary sequence of events that affect a person in the course of their life. According to the deterministic principle, each event is a necessary consequence of the respective pre-conditions. Regardless of the subjective *quality* of the events that affect them, every person faces an inevitable fate. However, the erroneous equation of the terms "cause" and "purpose" is problematic.

This can be attributed to the lack of linguistic differentiation of the word "reason". Thus, if one speaks of the reasons for an event, then this can only refer to the actual *causes*. If, on the other hand, purposes are interpreted in such a way that they serve as explanations for events, then it leads to a false conclusion and results in superstition. In earlier times, people also believed that sacrificing animals brought a good harvest and that higher powers would punish them with poor harvests (purpose) if they failed to do so. It is, of course, different with any events in the interpersonal sphere. Here, goal-oriented action plays a central role.

Some people, based on their religious convictions, believe that they are being "tested," so to speak, by certain events. If something bad happens to them (from their perspective), they believe that the event has the *purpose* to test their faith or to teach them a certain lesson. To them, this is the "reason" for the event (focus on purpose).

An atheist would not make such a consideration, because they do not believe in a power that purposefully influences their life. Thus, for them, only the analysis of the true causes of the event is possible, which is why they can prevent a repetition of the event and do not feel unjustified guilt. For them, the reason of an event lies only in the causes that led to the event, not in a hypothetical purpose.

The reason for an apple to fall from a tree is its mass and the law of gravity, which pulls it towards the surface of the earth. It would be wrong to say that the reason is the "intention" of the tree to reproduce through the seeds contained in the apple. In determinism there are—apart from the actions of humans and animals—no events that follow a planned course of action, i.e. that are directed towards a specific goal. Events do not proceed in a certain way because they are deliberately guided. Instead, the laws of nature determine the results of all processes in the universe.

In practical terms, this means that humans can justifiably hope to influence events. Of course, they can never be sure that their actions will have any real effect on the outcome. However, this realisation also prevents a discouraged attitude, which can arise from fatalism. In determinism, a person knows that they are helping to shape their inevitable destiny.

Every action, however small, can be an important impulse in life. In fatalism, on the other hand, a person mistakenly believes that in the end, it does not matter what they do, because fate is predefined *independently* of their actions. A seriously ill determinist therefore assumes that it is already certain if they will recover. Nevertheless, they will see the doctor, because this action *could* be important for the desired, positive result. Of course, the doctor may not be able to help, but nobody can know that. The fatalist, on the other hand, is convinced that they will die or survive, whether they go to the doctor or not.

3.23 Religion

The quality of religion is based on offering simple answers to complicated and sometimes unfathomable questions, and thus justifying one's own existence. It provides moral rules of conduct and suggests a certain world view to the believer. Especially when it comes to the question of whether one's own actions are right or wrong, many people feel unable to find a reliable and certain answer. Instead of defining moral behaviour themselves, people can resort to religion and follow its ideas. Whether or not the rules of conduct defined as *right* are followed depends on the will of the person and their ability to influence it through education.

Religion gives a clearly defined meaning to life, but —in the absence of an objective meaning to life— can only be based on ultimately arbitrary convictions and teachings. Quite contrary to the believer's expectations, the actual effect of religion only shows itself in the physical world and not in an existence after death. Religions are therefore propositions of faith that always refer to the truth and lay claim to universal validity. However, they have no basis in the natural world.

In addition to this, religions often provide explanations for events that are difficult to analyse by scientific methods. This particularly includes the origin of the world or the universe. A statement that is as widespread as it is false is the assertion that non-believers would trace the origin of the universe back to a giant →coincidence because they do not believe in a creator. The term coincidence itself is an irrational concept and serves—similar to the explanation of religion—as a kind of placeholder when no rational explanation can be found for a certain situation, according to the principle of cause and effect.

But even if the origin of the world, or *existence* itself, cannot be fully explained, this does not automatically mean that it is attributable to a supernatural force. The assumption that certain regularities were the determining factors here, too, is more reasonable than the assumption of a hypothetical god. It is in no way necessary to refute god (in the sense of a "primal force" or "first cause") in order to reject the teachings of any religion as unfounded.

Ultimately, all religious doctrines concerning human behaviour are based on dogmas that are arbitrarily established but attributed to a god. The special quality of religious teachings is justified by their belonging to a "holy scripture." However, it cannot be explained why one religion is preferred to all others. The mere fact that a Christian recognises the Bible but not the Hindu Bhagavad Gita as divine truth is enough for them to consider their faith as true and Hinduism as false. Thus, every believer is always an atheist as well, when it comes to all other religions and belief systems.

There are no compelling reasons and there is no necessity for the existence of god. But even if there is a god, this god—regardless of faith—obviously has no perceptible influence on our life and on our environment. All potentially meaningful elements within religious teachings arise from human interpretation of ancient or contemporary texts and are thus based on arbitrary assertions. These viewpoints are no more or less suitable than any other individual viewpoint to define the meaning of life or to separate good from evil.

Whether someone follows the alleged principles of a god or merely their own views in choosing their actions ultimately makes no significant difference. Moreover, hardly any other term is so unclearly defined as "god". Although some central characteristics tend to recur in the various interpretations, religions disagree on the details. If no clear definition of the phenomenon "god" can be presented, there is no need to consider its potential existence and the consequences resulting from it.

In practice, religion can have a stabilising and positive effect on individuals and communities. Ultimately, however, a certain price must always be paid for this security. The more a person alienates themselves from nature through religion and accepts unfounded teachings as truth, the more vulnerable they become to prejudice, manipulation and false conclusions. Through conscience, humans create an enemy in their own bodies, which tortures them whenever they violate the doctrines they have been taught.

Sex—by itself—does not suddenly become unpleasant just because it takes place before marriage. However, it will cause feelings of guilt in all those people who, due to their upbringing or their own conviction, tell themselves that marriage is the condition for this kind of affection. This is, however, completely superfluous when one considers that the justification for this rule can only be based on an arbitrary definition. A person with such a conviction will live against their biological tendency for no reason and unnecessarily suffer from conflicting desires. Something else, of course, is the renunciation of extramarital affairs, which a person imposes on themselves out of love and loyalty to their partner. The decisive aspect here is not an arbitrary set of beliefs, but the practically existing relationship with another person.

As a result, religion can lead to a variety of negative consequences. Depending on the type of religion and how it works, the risk of abuse can be very high. This is often reflected in the behaviour of certain sects. Just like a society, a religion can have very different effects. The more faith is in tune with human nature and the more compatible it is with the discoveries of science, the less harmful it is. Nevertheless, turning to religion and superstition cannot be recommended, since this step is ultimately always accompanied by a certain amount of misinformation. A seeking person will find all the answers they need in the surrounding nature. There, they can draw the truth straight from the source and are not dependent on arbitrary teachings.

4 Summary

At the end of the book, the most important state-ments concerning the practical side of mechanical philosophy are now repeated. They contain insights that have the greatest effect on human life. All are based on the principles explained before. This last section also contains new and more far-reaching conclusions, which were not yet formulated or only hinted at in the previous chapters. For this reason, the summary also serves as a collection of advice and suggestions which, in themselves, should provide the most comprehensive overview possible.

- There is no coincidence, only a lack of cer-tainty. Attributing an event to chance means not recognising the real causes of that event.

- The distinction between natural and artificial things is based on arbitrary criteria. Man has never left the realm of nature and therefore cannot create anything that cannot be defined as natural.

- Judgements about positive or negative events only arise through human interpretation. Nothing is perceived as good or bad by itself, except pleasure and pain.

- Personal happiness requires nothing more than the own conviction of being happy. However, this does not mean that it is easy to reach this state.

- Every person has a different physique and a different psyche. All the differences that make people think, feel and act differently necessarily arise from this basis.

- Not only is it impossible to act against one's own will, the thought itself is illogical. Every decision originates from the will, independently from the respective influencing factors.

- The influence of humans on themselves and their environment is very limited. This makes all worries about events out of our control unnecessary. They will happen anyway and we cannot do anything about it.

- The will is never free. No human being can choose their path to personal happiness or their way of perception.

- Every human strives for pleasure. Only the personal differences between people are the reasons why this pleasure is hidden behind different disguises.

- The amount of pleasure and pain received is the only criterion for judging actions.

- A person's state of mind is the result of striving for pleasure minus the negative feelings caused by one's own actions. The aim is always to maximise pleasure and minimise suffering.

- Every improvement in quality of life leads to a habituation effect over time. A noticeable increase in happiness can only be achieved by further raising the standard, although this is increasingly difficult to achieve. Contentment becomes permanent when people do not take anything of the good that already surrounds them for granted.

- A person who regularly imagines losing what is important to them has two advantages: On the one hand, they appreciate these things more, and on the other hand, they are better prepared should they actually lose them.

- Everything good in life can be lost at any time, including life itself. As in so many other situations, people are usually not able to prevent this.

- Excesses are attempts to maintain an impossible standard of pleasure. Short phases of pleasure are compensated by the inevitable failure of these attempts.

- Excessively positive expectations can easily be disappointed, while excessively negative expectations create suffering without any harm done. By keeping expectations as realistic as possible, combined with an optimistic view of the actual results, we are doing ourselves the best service.

- Self-interest is the only true driving force for human action. Every action is only carried out because of the positive effects it has on the human being. No one can escape this effect, which is why this self-interested attitude is to be considered morally neutral from an objective point of view.

- Although humans pursue goals in a rational way, their lives themselves do not follow a purposeful strategy to achieve an objectively justifiable goal in life. Any opinion about a meaning of life is ultimately based on arbitrariness and cannot be generalised.

- If there is no objective meaning of life, a life can never fail. Because if there is no "right", there is no "wrong". This frees humans from great pressure, for which there is no reasonable justification.

- The meaning of individual events disappears in view of our whole life. The meaning of our life disappears in view of the whole universe.

- Every human being is already perfect in every moment, at least as perfect as they can be at a given instance. If a person can only follow one path in life, it is impossible to deviate from it, and mistakes are ruled out.

- If each person is regarded as an individual, one can no longer judge their characteristics. Only in comparison with others do these characteristics appear as weaknesses or as advantages.

- What has happened cannot be undone, only acceptance remains. Remorse, anger and feelings of guilt are useless, because they cannot change the past. Instead, they unnecessarily create additional suffering. The only possibility left is to make a better decision next time.

- Sometimes short-term setbacks have a positive effect in the long run. Even obstacles on the way can later prove to be important milestones.

- If a person is satisfied with their current situation, they should not doubt their past. All past events were necessary to reach the place where they are today.

- Every being always chooses the action that seems to be the best possible option at any given moment. Even if the decision made is already regretted in the next second, it was the only possible choice for the time being. Therefore, it is absurd to regret one's actions.

- Self-pity is extremely harmful to the person's well-being in the long run, as it fuels their own conviction of being a victim. Through

the subjective impression of having experienced suffering, the suffering becomes real.
This way of thinking should therefore be
avoided at all costs.

- The opinions of other people cannot be controlled. It is not advisable to make one's own
happiness dependent on the approval of others.

- Humans should direct their attention mainly
to the present. While the past can no longer
be changed, the future cannot yet be reliably
influenced. Planning makes sense and
should be done, but present events can ruin
all planning.

- Without free will there is no absolute guilt.
However, there is the relative accountability
of the individual for their actions. Even if a

person does not bear objective guilt for their actions, they can still be stopped.

- Since human beings are basically able to reflect on the consequences of their actions, incentives and punishments can work. For this reason, it can be useful to punish people for certain actions. However, these punishments should be measured by their usefulness, while mere acts of revenge should be avoided.

- Both society and the individual have a legitimate interest in protecting themselves. This also includes punitive measures and self-defence.

- All human abilities, characteristics and even possessions ultimately stem from the gifts of nature. In conjunction with the non-existence of free will, this has fundamental implications for the perception of a just society.

5 Epilogue

The origins of the mechanical philosophy go back to the 17th century, although it did not reach its peak until the 18th century. Some of its central ideas, however, are—as mentioned at the beginning—still significantly older and are attributed to some philosophers from ancient Greece. However, scientific progress from the end of the 19th century and later led science to turn away from the image of the universe as a gigantic machine and instead to look for new explanations and theories.

The question arises, however, whether the mechanical world view may still be suitable for describing the functioning of processes in the universe, at least in a simplified form. Systems theory turned against the alleged reductionism (i.e. the isolated consideration of individual elements without regard to their interconnection in a whole) in the mechanical world view and demanded a holistic approach. But how could mechanical philosophy be thought at all if it did not necessarily include the natural and determined interactions of all events and objects with each other?

Other theories arose because mankind reached the limit of its ability to understand. Chaos research, which is essentially concerned with the *predictability* of processes, found that even the slightest changes in the initial conditions or in the course of processes can lead to massive effects in terms of the result and the process of events. This finding is in no way contradictory to the mechanistic world view. The currently prevailing interpretation of quantum mechanics (i.e. the field of mechanics in which the behaviour of particles at the subatomic level is studied) assumes that quantum physical processes are *not determined*. However, it cannot be ruled out that the apparent contradiction with determinism is attributable to limited human measuring methods rather than to an actual indeterminism.

The criticism of mechanical philosophy from these directions shows that arguments against its practical conclusions are going nowhere. For even if the existence of indeterminism were to prove itself in the end, it is unlikely that it would be capable of providing people with free will. Certainly, the mechanistic world view itself has been unjustifiably reduced and simplified beyond recognition in the context of this criticism. The frequent conflation of determinism and the predictability of events is largely responsible for the misinterpretation of mechanical philosophy.

Even if humans find it difficult to accept their own limitations, it must be clear that there will always be phenomena for which no reliable explanation can be provided. But to ignore those regularities considered to be certain on a macroscopic level just for the sake of a conclusive theory cannot be the right way to a consistent, practical view of the world. Of course, science will always make new and more far-reaching discoveries, but regardless: Mechanical philosophy is still capable of freeing humans from their primitive exceptionalism (i.e. the conviction of uniqueness in relation to the rest of nature). Although they represents the most intelligent life form in the world, they cannot claim any special position for themselves.

Not least the remaining hope of some people that perhaps they do carry a divine spark within them or to even save free will might have tipped the scales in favour of an escape from the universe as clockwork. However, people cannot commit themselves to only half of nature. A practical analysis forces us to face the fact: We are living machines that move through life as if we were on rails. Knowing this and nature itself, it is up to us to make our lives as fulfilling and beautiful as possible.

6 Notes on the 3rd Edition

The original version of this book was first published in 2020 and has subsequently been revised. Apart from replacing the cover, the text has been improved and errors were corrected. The 3rd edition, however, was dedicated to a different goal.

The text passages in the earlier editions that mixed the concepts of *psychological* and *ethical* hedonism were subjected to an examination and were clarified accordingly. It became clear that the mere fact that every living being (and thus also humans) uses the generation of pleasure and pain to evaluate actions cannot serve as a justification for a normative *ethical* hedonism. In contrast to the viewpoint repeatedly presented in this book that morality has no basis beyond the subjective perception of human beings, ethical hedonism is one of the moral theories that defend an *objective* standard for moral actions. This consists of adherence to the pleasure principle, with consideration for all living beings involved (exception: egoistic hedonism).

However, considering the origin and role of morality in human societies, this appears to be a false conclusion. Accordingly, being moral does not mean maximising the sum of the well-being of all concerned, but merely to act according to certain convictions for reasons of one's own pleasure. This statement has been clarified in the current, 3rd edition of the book.